500
BEST IRISH JOKES
AND LIMERICKS

illustrated by Doug Anderson

BELL PUBLISHING COMPANY • NEW YORK

Introduction

On a Wednesday night in August, Joey Bishop told an NBC-TV audience that "It was so hot today I saw a tree chasing a dog." Later on he told about his Jewish uncle who went to the doctor with a mysterious crick in his neck. "Have you ever had it before?" asked the doctor. The uncle nodded. "So, you have it again," diagnosed the doctor.

Both jokes were born in Ireland, a joke factory if ever a country was one. The witticism of Galway today is the wisecrack of Las Vegas in two or three years. The famous sex researcher Dr. Kinsey is reported to have given a wisecrack that was originally told at Trinity College some 80 years ago.

The greatest wits have been Irish: Swift, Sheridan, Wilde, Shaw. Even the humor and satire of the early Irish bards were well known. Dr. Johnson said: "The Irish are a very truthful race. They never speak well of one another." In the world at large everything may be serious, but not hopeless, while in Ireland everything may be hopeless, but not serious.

As far as limericks go, they would seem to have originated in the County of the same name. The meter is an ancient one in the Irish language; examples from the eighth century are to be found. Though they are now often bawdy, they began clean as a Sunday hymn. The "Song of the Sea" by Rumann MacColmain, written in the eighth century, went like this:

> When the wind comes from the south,
> Over the shield-bearing Saxons stout
> It drives waves up Skiddy
> Makes high Calad Nit giddy,
> Pounding the grey-green of Shannon's mouth.

That's a long way from "There once was a girl from Kilpedder." Two leading experts, one Irish and one Italian, agree that the earthiness of the limerick as we know it stems from the form's unconscious but powerful biological rhythm.

It will help the Irish joke reader to know that Nationalists are usually Roman Catholic, Orangemen and Unionists are Protestant. In the Republic of Ireland the police force is called the Garda Siochana, or Civic Guard. Poteen is an illegal distilled spirit not uncommon in the west of Ireland. Gaelic is still the language of the home in several areas and Irish words like "amadan" (fool) and "slainte" (health) are used to flavor English speech.

Sean Maire came into the garage, walked up to the parking space and, squatting down, went through the motions of driving a car.

'Horan,' said a shocked customer, 'why don't you tell the man he hasn't a car.'

'Is it mad you take me for? Sure he pays me a pound to wash it every time he comes in.'

It was Padraig's first day in the Waterford glass factory.

'Padraig,' asked the foreman, 'did you mark the top of all those crates with the notice "This side up with care?"'

'Deed, I did, Mr O'Sullivan, and I put it on the bottom as well to make sure.'

Then there was the Kildare woman who wrote home from Paris saying it was lovely to hear the French pheasants singing the Mayonnaise.

A colleen of fair Ballycrotty,
Loved men of all colours—'twas dotty,
   But her children's a sight,
   Every heart to delight,
For they're black, brown, green-striped and half spotty.

Two little girls were talking about religious knowledge.

'I'm past Original Sin,' boasted the first one.

'That's nothing,' answered the other. 'I'm beyond Redemption.'

'We are now passing the premises of Arthur Guinness, the largest brewery in the world,' said the guide to his busload of tourists.

'I'm damned if we are,' cried Smith as he hopped off.

A Belfast newspaper once reported the launching of an aircraft carrier and recorded: 'The Duchess smashed the bottle against the bow and amid the applause of the crowd she slid on her greasy bottom into the sea.'

Paudge, Liam and Francis were shifting furniture but when Paudge struggled with a huge oak wardrobe he noticed that Liam was missing.

'Francis, where's Liam? He should be helping us with this.'

'And sure so he is,' protested Francis. 'He's inside holding the clothes hangers in place.'

'Paddy, how is it that whenever you ask an Irishman a question he always answers with another?'

'Who told you that?'

The Boyle carrier was asked to send in his bill for doing a few jobs with his horse and cart. It came as follows: '*Three comes and three goes at ten shillings a went—three pounds.*'

The blind farmer was often taken for a walk in the fields by a kind neighbour. However kindly the neighbour might have been he was undoubtedly a coward. When a bull charged towards them one day he abandoned the blind man.

The bull, puzzled by a lack of fear, nudged the farmer in the back. He turned very quickly, caught the bull by the horns and threw it to the ground with a bump that left it breathless.

'Aidan,' said the neighbour, 'I never knew you were so strong.'

'Faith, and if I could have got that fella off the handlebars of the bicycle I'd have thrashed him properly.'

For Hippies and Beats the Fleadh Ceoil,
Brings alcohol bliss to the soul,
    A Hippie to fill,
    Takes twelve pints and a gill,
While six bars to each Beat is their goal.

Aonghus decided to keep a few hives on his farm and the first year Eoin was curious to know how he got on.

'Had you any luck with the bees, Aonghus?' he asked.

'The best . . . the best,' Aonghus chuckled.

'You got a lot of honey?'

'Not a drop—but they stung the mother-in-law seven times.'

Then there was the notice outside an Irish dance hall which proclaimed that 'Ladies and gentlemen are welcome, regardless of sex.'

A dieting girleen named Flynn,
Reduced until she was thin.
    She's no more, I'm afraid,
    For she sipped lemonade,
And slipped through the straw to fall in.

3

A lovely young maid of Kilglass,
Wore intimate garments of brass.
Pat, one night on the porch,
With acetylene torch,
Just melted resistance, alas!

The Civic Guard was very anxious to discover where the poteen was being made, so he kept after Conan who was known to carry out repairs to stills.

'Come on, Conan,' he pleaded, 'just tell me where you repaired the still.'

'I will, Guard Clancy,' said Conan blandly, 'I will.'

'Where then? Tell me.'

'To tell you the living truth, Guard, I mended it where the hole was.'

Strolling through Ireland's supreme honeymoon resort, Glen-garriff, Francis Xavier Muldoon was a picture of bliss.

'But, Muldoon,' asked the local barkeeper, 'how is it you come here on your honeymoon without the wife?'

'Are you mad, man?' said Muldoon, 'Sure if she came, who'd look after the shop?'

There's a saying in Northern Ireland which is used when they want to hint at the destination of some departed scoundrel. 'Ah, sure the mon's gone to a place where he'll be able to light his pipe with his finger.'

He had been waiting a long time for his train at an out-of-the-way Galway railway station.

'Look,' he complained to the station-master, 'I'm fed up with this. Could you give me the time the trains are supposed to run each day. Have you a timetable?'

'Timetable is it? Bless your sense. It's a calendar we use here.'

A new Bishop had been appointed to an Australian diocese where the Irish predominated. He was perturbed to discover that almost all the churches were named after Irish saints—St Patrick, St Brigid, St Declan and so on. At the first opportunity he dedicated a church to St Athanasius in order to change the pattern. Inevitably a deputation of his flock came to see him.

'Well,' asked the Bishop, 'and what can I do for you?'

'Nothing much, Your Lordship,' they answered, 'but we want to know what St Athanasius ever did for Ireland?'

'O'Dubhgaill, this cheque is crossed. I can't pay it over the counter.'

'All right, I'll come around behind so.'

There was a young lady of Siam,
Who said to her lover Priam,
'You can kiss me, of course,
But it must be by force,
For God knows you are stronger than I am.'

It was late at night and Gill was looking for something under a street lamp.

'What are you looking for?' asked the kindly *Garda*.

'I lost my wallet down the street and I'm searching for it.'

'But if you lost it down the street what are you searching here for?'

'Sure there's more light.'

'I believe you had a terrible fight with Murphy.'

'I had, too, and I'd have licked him only I was stopped getting at him.'

'Who stopped you?'

'Murphy.'

A bookseller toiling in Drogheda,
Had an assistant who often annogheda.
Complaints came in volumes,
And were stacked up in columns,
So she wished she had never emplogheda.

They were an innocent honeymoon couple right from the heart of Connemara and they were shown to their hotel room. It had twin beds.

'Oh, Colum,' wailed the bride, 'why can't we have a room to ourselves.'

The circus elephant was dead and the three men sat glumly and sad on the wagon outside his tent.

'I know the elephant is a big loss,' said the clown, 'but why do you three take it so bad?'

'We've got to dig the grave!'

They drove towards the city in zig-zag pattern.
'Shamus, ish we near Dublin yet?'
'Yesh. We're knocking down more people so we mush be.'
'Drive slower then.'
'Whadda ya mean, drive slower? You're driving.'

'Why are you giving me a dirty look, Mrs Behan?'
'I didn't give you a dirty look. You had it when you came.'

The farmer was plainly in difficulty with his horse. He wrestled with the reins to stop him and he flapped them wildly to get him to start.

'Look,' said Smith, an English tourist, 'why don't you say "Whoa" when you want him to stop and "get up" when you want him to go?'

'Listen to me,' said the farmer, 'that horse kicked me three years ago and if you think I'm going to go asking him for favours you're mistaken.'

Then there was the Irish shopkeeper who said his eggs were so fresh the hens hadn't missed them.

In Dublin's Moore Street the American tourist picked up a melon and jokingly asked the stall-holder:

'Say, is this the biggest apple you can grow around here?'

She turned with cool cynicism and calmly told him, 'Buy that grape or put it down.'

There was an Old Man of the Dargle,
Who purchased six barrels of Gargle;
   For he said, 'I'll sit still,
   And roll them down the hill,
For the fish in the depths of the Dargle.'

In the midst of a downpour Earnain and Shamus took their captive landlord to shoot him.

'Isn't it terrible,' wailed the victim, 'to shoot a man in weather like this.'

'What about us?' said Shamus indignantly. 'You don't have to walk back in it.'

Murphy was complaining to the sergeant about the bread.

'There's nothing wrong with that bread,' said the sergeant. 'A hundred years ago the people of Ireland would have been thrilled to have bread like that.'

'I know,' said Murphy, 'but it was fresh then.'

A great Irish thinker named Berkeley,
Expressed his beliefs, oh, so starkly.
   'Almost all that we see,
   Cannot possibly be,
And the rest I conceive is unlarkly.'

On a tombstone in Kilmurry, Co. Clare, there's an inscription:

This stone was raised by Sarah's lord,
Not Sarah's virtues to record
For they're well known to all the town,
But it was raised to keep her down.

'I don't know what I'll do with the wife asking for ten pounds now and five pounds again.'

'In the name of St Kieran, what does she do with the money?'

'I couldn't tell you. I never give it to her.'

'O'Mara,' protested the farmer to his labourer, 'aren't you a bit too dirty. Did you never think of having a wash?'

'That's not fair,' protested O'Mara. 'I may not wash very often but I never let a day go by without giving meself a good dust.'

Said Murphy to Quinn: 'Nature is wonderful. Look at the way she puts cream at the top of the milk so that people can get it.'

Said Quinn to Burke: 'The field was that muddy they had to dig tunnels to milk the cows.'

Some merry old monks of Manulla,
Found life was becoming much dulla.
     They brewed a fine ale,
     In a massive big pail,
And they and their lives were much fulla.

It was a typical shop selling Roman Catholic religious goods and there were many statues of the saints. With savage energy, a Protestant Orangeman shattered them with his stick.

In court he explained why.

'Me Lord. I couldn't pass the place by and not do something. If there's one thing I hate, it's bigotry.'

The stout was awful and the farmer complained bitterly to the owner of the public-house.

'What are you complaining about?' said the barkeeper indignantly. 'You've only got a pint but I've got 78 barrels of the awful stuff.'

A lover of old in fair Gort,
Had two arms that were powerful but short,
    When for girls he would reach,
    He was forced to choose each,
From the narrow and spanable sort.

The new recruit to the Irish army wrote home to his family on the farm: *'The army life is lovely and they let us lie in until 6.30 am.'*

Dempsey stood at the edge of the magnificent Cliffs of Moher in Co. Clare when his son came up to him.

'Daddy,' he said, 'Mammy says you're to come away from the cliffs or give me the sandwiches for lunch.'

You'll find in our Irish cheese
Aphrodisiac qualities.
   Its remarkable curds,
    Are praised beyond wurds,
By both sexes, the he's and the she's.

'Mrs O'Shaughnessy, could you give me anything for a home for alcoholics?'

'Come back at teatime. My husband will be in then.'

And we should not forget the Irishman who said he would rather die than be buried in a Protestant cemetery.

Two Dublin girls met and compared notes on their holidays.

'Where d'ya go, Anasthasia?'

'I went to Majorca.'

'Where's that?'

'I don't know. We flew.'

A western young lady named Flynn,
Would tell of her plans with a grin,
   'I intend to be bold,
   In manner untold,
For there's need of original sin.'

'That was a terrible storm ye had down your way, Paudge.'
''Twas surely. Our hen had her back to the wind and she laid the same egg five times.'

The travelling show had a knife-throwing act and Mulligan went twice to see the fascinating spectacle. When Flaherty told him that he was going, he didn't encourage him.
'Don't, Flaherty,' he said, 'you'll be wasting your money.'
'How's that?'
'He has a rotten aim. He keeps missing her.'

Peadar had been to the mission at the local church.
'What had the missioner to talk about, Paudeen?'
'Sin.'
'What did he say about it?'
'He doesn't agree with it.'

The motorist was honest and when he hit the cock wandering on the road he stopped and went back to the cottage.
'I'm afraid I killed your cock, Madam, but I'd very much like to replace him.'
'Whatever you want,' said the sour-pussed farmer's wife, 'go around the side there and you'll find the hens in the back.'

She gave the tinker a sixpenny piece with a great flourish.
'There, it gives me great pleasure to give you that.'
He looked at it.
'Give us five bob, mam, and have a real good time.'

A lively young fellow named Kelly,
Got an awful sad ache in his digestion.
   His wife in her haste,
   Had served him up paste,
Instead of the blancmange and jelly.

He was showing the visitors the historical places of the area as he drove the bus.

'Here in Ballynastraffan we beat the British in 1641 . . .'
They moved on.

'The Irish thrashed the base, brutal and bloody Saxon here in 1798 . . .'
A little further.

'On this spot, ladies and gentlemen, one hundred and twenty years ago we knocked the unholy lard out of a crowd of British redcoats in spite of all their treachery could do.'

An English tourist grew understandably irate.

'Look,' he said, 'surely the British must have beaten the Irish some place or other?'

The driver glared.

'Not on this bus, anyway,' he growled.

A ghost in the town of Macroom,
One night found a ghoul in his room.
   They argued all night,
   As to which had the right,
To frighten the wits out of whom.

The speaker in Hyde Park put it strong. 'Show me an Irishman,' he said, 'and I'll show you a coward!'

Colm Flynn stepped out of the crowd and flexed his vast muscles.

'I'm showing you an Irishman,' he said threateningly.

'Take a look at a coward,' said the speaker hastily as he set off at Olympic speed.

The *Garda* watched Mulligan desperately trying to open his front door as he swayed from side to side.

'Here, Mulligan,' he said, 'can I help you with that key?'

'Nosh at all, Guard. I can manage the key if you—hic—could hold the house steady.'

A miserly farmer of Nenagh,
Grew daily more leanagh and leanagh.
    He remained undistressed,
    Though his back touched his chest,
For the money he saved made him meanagh.

'My father pays our rent,' complained Mrs Carey to her husband, 'my mother buys our clothes and my aunt pays for our groceries. My brother helps with the children's school fees and my sister arranges our holidays. I'm ashamed that we can't do better.'

'I know how you feel,' soothed her husband. 'Sure you have at least two uncles who give us nothing.'

'Hey, Mick, will you hurry up. Haven't you an appointment with Kieran?'

'I have, but I told him I'd be late so I've lots of time yet.'

The dentist was shocked by Mikeen's teeth.

'From now on,' he said, 'you'll have to brush them often and use toothpaste.'

'Toothpaste, is it? Sure there's not one of them loose.'

Stacey returned home after his first holiday abroad and he didn't look too happy.

'Did you enjoy yourself?' asked his neighbour.

'Well to tell you the truth, I'm so glad to be home I'm not sorry I went.'

Maguire's relations were too fond of dropping in for meals. On one occasion he had a lot of them in and he gave them exceptionally large helpings of pork.

"Twas grand, Maguire, 'twas grand,' said his first cousin once removed.

'It should have been,' answered Maguire, 'that was none of your slaughtered meat. That pig met a natural death.'

Said a silly old boyo of Sneem,
'My telly is powered by hot steam.
  The reception is vile,
  But when brought to the bile,
It gives tea—if not V—that's a dream.'

Shaun was a noted drinker in the village. At intervals he became a teetotaller and took what is known in Ireland as 'the pledge'.

'Well, Shaun,' asked the curate who was new to the place, 'how long do you want to take it for?'

'It's easy to see you're new, Father. Sure everyone knows I never take it for anything less than life.'

'Have you wild duck?'

'Well, no then, but we could annoy a tame one for you.'

'Tis famous, the food of Killarney,
As tasty and fresh as sweet Blarney.
　　Knowing well it is nice
　　When served fast on ice,
Gourmets shriek for the Chilly Con Kearney.

The Coventry landlady politely asked her new lodger from Clare
if he'd like his eggs on toast. Equally polite and accommodating,
he answered: 'Well, mam, if you haven't got a plate they'll do
that way.'

The American had been fishing for two weeks at Ballinahinch
without getting a bite. On the last day of his vacation he caught
a small salmon.

'Turlough,' he said to his gillie as the fish was gaffed, 'that
salmon cost me five hundred dollars.'

'Well now sir,' comforted Turlough, 'aren't you the lucky
man you didn't catch two.'

There was an Old Person of Down,
Whose face was adorned with a frown;
　　When he opened the door,
　　For one minute or more,
He alarmed all the people of Down.

The farmer's cow was stolen and he was complaining loudly. His cousin from Dublin consoled him.

'Don't worry, Phelim. They can't get far with it. Didn't I see you drain its fuel tank last night.'

Slattery swung his sledge hammer with cheerful abandon and struck his workmate a fearful thump on the side of the head.

'Slattery, Slattery, be careful,' begged Donegan, 'you're after making me bite my lip.'

> A handsome young boyo named Pat,
> With girls would enjoy this and that.
> He meant to cuddle and kiss,
> When he spoke about 'this,'
> Just guess what he meant by his 'that.'

The Irish missionary was preaching to the African tribe.

'And I say to you that you must love your fellowmen!'

'Moolagumbi!' shrieked the natives.

'White man and black man must learn to co-operate.'

'Moolagumbi!' chanted the crowd.

The missionary was very pleased and he told the chief how pleased he was with the reception.

'I am glad, O man of Ireland,' said the chief, 'but be careful as we pass my cattle that you do not step into the moolagumbi.'

One optimistic farmer in Co. Offaly gave hot water to his hens. He wanted them to lay boiled eggs.

Carson, the barrister and politician, asked a reluctant witness:

'Is it true, miss, that you are a prostitute?'

'That's my business,' was the indignant reply.

'I see, well please tell the court your hobbies.'

Then there was the Irishman who was asked the difference between an explosion and a collision. 'In a collision,' he replied, 'there you are but in an explosion where are you?'

There was an old man of Kilkenny,
Who squandered each week just one penny.
   He often would swank,
   Of his wealth in the bank,
It was one way to save, *nota bene*.

It was the end of a long friendship as Dara and Killian said good-bye.

'Dara, when I'm in Australia will you come to the pub and have two drinks, one for me and one for you in memory of old times.'

'I will too, Killian. And you'll do the same for me.'

'I will that, Dara.'

And so night after night Dara went through the ritual. One large Irish for himself and then another for Killian in Australia.

Came the day, however when he ordered only one drink. The barman was curious.

'If ye'll forgive me intrusion, Dara, why have you given up one of the drinks.'

'Simple, oul son, simple. I'm on the wagon now.'

Kelly staggered back on board his ship drunk as could be.

'Kelly,' said the officer, 'it's a great pity you drink. If you'd been sober you might have become a second officer like me. Think of what drink cost you.'

'Nonsense,' muttered Kelly, 'sure when I get a few drinks I'm an admiral.'

'Liam, your uncle is on the phone and he wants to know is the new child a boy or a girl.'

'Well now, will you ask the poor bothered man what else it could have been.'

'That will be five pounds or a month in jail,' the judge said sharply.

'Very well, sir,' said Flaherty, 'I'll take the five pounds.'

'Mary, what we need in our hotel is a chef.'

'Sure what good would he be?'

'I tell you that some of them are so clever they can give a different name to the same soup every day of the week.'

Mrs Keogh was looking out the window.

'Tommy,' she said, 'there's Mulcahy home and he's drunk again.'

'How do you know?'

'He's putting a penny in the post box, looking at his watch and shouting to everyone that he's lost seven stone.'

A cute curate who lived in Dundalk,
Proclaimed he could fly like a hawk,
    Cheered by thousands of people,
    He leapt from a steeple,
But the splash-down proved it was just talk.

When she opened the door a forlorn tinker stood on the door-step.

'Please, me good woman, could you spare me a bit of creamy cake?'

She was shocked.

'Now, wouldn't bread be much better for you?'

He shuffled his feet: 'I know, mam. But today's me birthday.'

Two Canadians—one huge and the other very tiny—were cutting down a tree with a crosscut saw under the indignant eye of Seoirse. Finally he could stand it no longer as he watched them pull the saw backwards and forwards. He hit the biggest one a straight right to the chin.

'You big bully,' he yelled, 'give it to the little fella if he wants it.'

'Mrs Heffernan,' complained the new girl, 'your husband tries to hold me and kiss me.'

'Don't worry about that,' said Mrs Heffernan. 'He was like that with me after we got married but he gets over it very quickly.'

O'Gorman jumped up from the card table white with rage.

'Stop this game,' he shouted, 'Fitzgerald is cheating!'

'How do you know?'

'He's not playing the hand I dealt him.'

Mrs Mulligan brought her dear departed husband's photograph to the dealer.

'Could you enlarge this?'

'Certainly, madam.'

'And could you remove his hat?'

'We could touch it up for you—but which side was his hair parted?'

'Is it mad you are! Sure won't you see that when you take off his hat!'

An Irish alibi is the proof that you were in two places at the one time.

Darragh was boasting of his grandfather: 'He lived for ninety-four years and never once used glasses.'

'He had the right of it,' nodded Phelim. 'I always said it was healthier to drink from the bottle.'

'Hey, Paudge, do I hear you spitting in the vase on the mantelpiece?'

'No, Brigid, but I'm getting closer all the time.'

The puritan people of Teeling,
Express all their horror with feeling.
　　When they see that a chair,
　　Has all its legs bare,
They look away straight to the ceiling.

They got jammed in the restaurant door and Peadar used some unconstitutional language which annoyed Liam.

'How dare you swear before my wife,' he protested.

'I'm sorry,' said Peadar with contrition, 'I didn't know she wanted to swear first.'

An advertisement appeared in a Wicklow newspaper: *'Young farmer would like to hear from young woman with tractor with a view to matrimony. Please send picture of the tractor.'*

An artist bizarre of Clonsast,
With his work made the public aghast,
　　'Til they burned it in pits,
　　With this crack from the wits,
'His art's in the right place at last.'

The doctor was puzzled.

'I'm very sorry but I can't diagnose your trouble, Mahoney. I think it must be drink.'

'Don't worry about it, Dr. Kelly, I'll come back when you're sober.'

Said a wicked old man of Kilkee,
'With her big toe my wife stirs her tea.
　　It's true that I let her,
　　Tho' I could do better,
But what if the neighbours should see?'

An old lady was impressed by the sermons of the missioner and she told a friend about him.

'Do you know,' she said, 'he can preach about Hell as if he was born and reared in the place.'

Father Burke, a famous member of a Catholic religious order, was in the witness box many years ago. The cross-examining counsel was tough as he could be, but his efforts broke on the gaiety of the priest. Finally he turned to personal remarks.

'What is that peculiar thing on your head?" he asked, referring to the round, flat skullcap worn by Father Burke.

'That, sir,' came the reply, 'is the case for the crown.'

They met after the new baby had been christened.

'What did you call her, Mam?'

'Hazel.'

'Are you daft! With an Irish saint's name for every day of the week, you have to call her after a nut.'

'Do you like Irish Punch?' asked Michael of his French friend.

'Certainement,' shrugged Pierre, 'but eez a contradiction.'

'A contradiction?'

'You put in ze whiskey to make it strong: you add ze water to make it weak: ze sugar to make it sweet and ze lemon to make it sour. Then you say "Here's to you!" and you drink it yourself.'

The following was a favourite story of Denis Ireland, the noted Ulster writer. The evening train from Ballymore was steaming quietly at the Parkmore terminal when the single passenger came up to talk to the driver.

'Will ye be takin' her oot the morrow, Wullie?'

'Aye, we mean to take her oot.'

'Well, ye needn't bother yersel'—ah'm not goin' to toon.'

'Mrs Hayes, your husband has made a remarkable recovery. He can get up and go out now.'

'Deed he can't. Sure didn't I sell his clothes when you told me he was finished.'

'Mary, you'll be surprised to know that your old boyfriend has asked me to marry him,' said Bridie with a smirk.

'Dear me, I knew he'd do something desperate.'

The neighbours were in for the wake and Mrs Gilhooly wanted to console the widow.

'You know, Mam, poor Willie looks grand and he all brown and sunburnt. Sure that holiday did him a powerful lot of good.'

A well-known Ballina hatter,
Had two sons as like as don't matter.
  To the former, he said:
  'Run along now to bed,'
But the young man replied, 'I'm the latter.'

He was a good lodger and Alf didn't want to get his Irish up too quickly but he couldn't tolerate it any longer.

'Look, Paddy, I don't wanna complain but will you flippin' well put down your boots a little quietly. Let's leave the ceiling up, mate.'

Paddy was contrite but as he was going to bed he forgot and threw one boot down with a crash. Immediately he realised his mistake and he put the other down gently. He had been asleep for an hour or two when he was awakened by a pounding on his door. It was his landlord.

'For blinkin' Pete's sake, Paddy, throw down that other boot . . .'

Country feuds in Ireland can be almost Sicilian in their vendetta qualities. A parish priest disgusted with the conduct of his flock addressed them from the pulpit.

'You're at each other's throats all the time. 'Tis a great pity ye are not heathens and you might start acting like Christians.'

There was an Old Person of Dundalk,
Who tried to teach fishes to walk:
    When they tumbled down dead,
    He grew weary and said,
'I had better go back to Dundalk.'

The doctor was not very good and his lady patient seemed to have a bad cold. Nothing he gave her was any use and she was growing dissatisfied.

'Can you do nothing to cure me, Doctor?'

'I tell you what to do,' he replied. 'Go home and have a hot bath and without drying yourself stand in the nude where there is a strong draught.'

'Will that cure me?' she asked with surprise.

'No, but it'll give you pneumonia and I can cure pneumonia.'

She was only a poteen maker's daughter but he loved her still.

Murphy couldn't understand how he'd injured his friend so much. As he told his wife: 'Heavens above, I had nothing in my hand when I hit him except my fist.'

The judges tried Pascal of Knock.
For wife murder he stood in the dock.
 He said to their faces,
 'I broke nuts with me braces,
And the oul' wan fell dead with shell-shock.'

'This is a quiet place,' said the tourist as he looked around the sleepy dusty square of the Cork town.
 'It wasn't always like that,' the local grimly remarked. 'I mind one time up in the hotel the serving man spilled a glass of wine on a woman and they hung him from the balcony you can see there. I though it was awful.'
 'You went to his aid, of course?'
 'I would have, only I was down in the kitchen kicking the skull of the cook because he hard-boiled me soft egg.'

'Mr Mullarkey,' asked the chemist, 'did that mudpack I asked you to try improve your wife's appearance?'
 'It did surely, but it keeps falling off.'

His monkey glands made poet, Yeats,
Most anxious with girls to have dates.
  His poetic measures,
  Gave very few pleasures,
If one can accept estimates.

'Why in the name of Heaven,' asked the weary passenger, 'did they build the railway station three miles from the village?'
'Ah,' nodded the porter, 'they must have thought it would be a good thing to have it near the trains.'

I'm afraid, Mrs Moylan, your husband will never work again,' aid the doctor sadly.
'I'll go in and tell him and it might cheer him up.'

A notice in a Galway newspaper some years ago is worthy of preservation: 'Because of lack of space a number of births have been held over until next week.'

'Mary, I heard you invited your boyfriend back to our apartment late at night. It worries me and your father.'
'It's all right, Ma. We went back to his place. Let his mother and father do the worrying.'

Drennan looked worried when he called on the psychiatrist.
"Tis like this,' he said. 'Me brother has something wrong with him. He's been thinking for months that he's a hen.'
'Glory be! Why didn't you come to me before this?'
'Ah, sure we needed the eggs.'

There was an old man of Tralee,
Who was bothered and bit by a flea,
So he put out the light,
Saying, 'Now he can't bite,
For he'll never be able to see.'

The honeymooners looked at the list of mealtimes in their hotel.

Breakfast 6.30 a.m. to 11.30 a.m.
Lunch 12.30 p.m. to 3.30 p.m.
Dinner 6.30 p.m. to 9.30 p.m.

'Kevin,' wailed the bride, 'sure we'll be in atin' so long we won't have time to go anywhere.'

A poetess living in Trim,
Possesses a peculiar whim,
She wears a large bonnet,
When writing a sonnet,
And a helmet when writing a hymn.

The customer put five shillings on the bar counter and staggered away. Colum put it in his pocket and turned to find the accusing eye of the boss glaring at him.

'Would you believe it at all,' Colum said blandly, 'he leaves a five shilling tip and doesn't pay for his drink!'

They were drunk after the annual college dinner and wanted to leave the hotel.

'Look, son. Howdjwegetout?'

The porter pointed along the passage.

'Turn to the right at the next passage and go down two steps and you'll be in the main hall.'

They staggered on together; turned right and fell down the lift shaft to the basement.

As they sorted themselves out Paddy rolled over.

'Look, Tadgh. If that fella thinks I'm going down the other step, he's crazy.'

> There was an old man of Kilbride,
> Who slipped in a sewer and died.
>> His stupid young brother,
>> Went into another,
> And the verdict on both was 'sewercide'.

The tinker put on a long look of misery as the farmer opened the door.

'The blessing of the saints on you, sir,' wailed the tinker, "tis I have been travelling the long white roads this day and the great emptiness inside me and the skin hanging about me the ways that a coat would hang on a pole. Sure, it's not you, sir, that would see a man starve?'

'I would not.' said the farmer coldly. 'I'd look away.'

The maid picked up the phone and muttered something before slamming it down.

'Who was that, Maire? I'm expecting a trunk call.'

'Only some mad idiot, Mr Slattery. He said it was a long distance from California. I told him we knew.'

A nun in a convent in Bray,
Saw her roses go into decay,
     Reverend Mother said, 'Dear,
     Please no longer fear,
Here's liquid manure, let us spray.'

Flannery was boasting about his cousin in America who was so big when he died that they couldn't get a coffin to fit him.

'Wasn't that extraordinary?' he asked.

Cummins was not impressed.

'Flannery,' he said, 'if they let the air out of your cousin they could have buried him in a matchbox.'

'Would you buy a raffle ticket for a poor widow?'

'Deed I won't. What would I do with her if I won?'

'I can't understand why Irish cream costs so much more than milk.'

'Simple. It's more expensive to train the cows to sit on small bottles.'

Another Brendan Behan story told of a good Dublin street dealer—they often wear big black enveloping shawls—who came down the road with one breast bare.

'Hey,' Brendan shouted at her. 'Make yourself decent.'

Her eyes popped as she swung the shawl about her and then the penny dropped: 'Holy Joseph, I left the baby on the bus.'

'Harnett, do you plead guilty?'

'I couldn't say, your Honour. I haven't heard the evidence yet.'

Quinn says there's nothing he wouldn't do for his mother-in-law and she says there's nothing she wouldn't do for him. It's true, too, Quinn says. They do nothing for each other.

There was a young lady of Oola,
Who waggled her hips in the Hula.
As she dropped her grass skirt,
She cried, 'I'm no flirt.
I've stripped to the buff to be coola.'

The teacher opened the letter that young Colm brought her.
Dear Teacher,
    Please stop giving Colm those sums about bottles of whiskey
at two shillings a bottle. It keeps his father awake at night . . .

'What's your name,' he asked the boy on the winding white
road to Fanad.
    'James Doherty.'
    'You should say "sir".'
    'All right. Sir James Doherty.'

A diner in cheery Belcoo,
Got a mouse in his Irish stoo.
    They said, 'My dear chap,
    Just fasten your trap,
You'll love the rich taste when you choo.'

The farmer showed the city labourer how to milk the cows and sent him into the fields.

'How many did you milk?' he asked when the labourer came back.

'Twenty, but there's one thing . . .'

'What's that?'

'I think you should have given me a bucket.'

He had killed the farmer's hen but he offered to pay for it.

'I'll give you a pound,' he assured the cottager.

'You'll have to make it two pounds,' said the old woman with a mournful shake of her head. 'Two of my fowls are destroyed by you.'

'What do you mean?' he asked indignantly.

'Ab when my cock finds out you killed that hen he'll die of shock.

'Was your father very shy, Ronan?'

'Shy? My mother told me that if he hadn't been so shy I'd be five years older now.'

Respect for the dead is a great Irish quality and when O'Reilly had to bury his mother-in-law he went round to the local to borrow something to do the thing decent.

'Lend us a tenner, Mr Ryan,' he pleaded.

Even publicans in Ireland respect the traditions and Casey searched the till to get the money.

'O'Reilly,' he said, 'I have only got nine pounds fourteen. Will that do?'

'It will. You can give me a pint of stout, five cigarettes and a razor blade to make up the difference.'

When Flaherty became a monk he was warned by the Abbot that the rule of silence was very strict. Three years after he was in it he asked for a carpenter to remove the huge nail sticking up through his plank bed and it was done. After five years more he asked for a glass of milk every day because an old stomach ulcer was acting up. Eight years after this he found he could stick the life no longer and told the Abbot he was leaving.

'Well,' said the Abbot, 'to tell you the truth I'm not surprised. You've been complaining ever since you joined.'

> There was young rose of Tralee,
> Who let herself go on a spree.
>   Now she writes to the papers,
>   Condemning such capers,
> And signs herself 'Mother of Three.'

Paddy strayed into a rather sleazy nightclub in London where the one big attraction was the strip dancer who performed in a cage with a lion. In the finale when she was down to her last sequin the moth-eaten lion placed its paws on her shoulders and licked her face.

'Well, Paddy,' said the club manager, 'could you do better than that?'

'Get that lion out of it, sir, and I'll have a try.'

Then there was the old lady who thought her horse was certain to win the Irish Derby because the bookie told her it would start at twenty to one and the race didn't begin until a quarter past.

> There was a young lady of Bandon,
> Whose feet were too narrow to stand on,
>   So she stood on her head,
>   'Til the day she was wed,
> Renowned for her reckless abandon.

'You're doing fine, Mullarkey and you tell me you're only playing golf for a month.'

'Oh, yes but it took me four years to learn.'

'Where are you going with that lantern, Paudeen?'
'I'm going out to meet me girl, Father.'
'I didn't take a lantern when I went courtin'.'
'I know, Father, but look what you got.'

A stupid young nitwit of Eire,
Would sit at his ease on a fire.
　　When told he was hot,
　　He would say he was not,
And heatedly call you a liar.

When her husband died Mrs O'Grady had a lot of trouble with the insurance company, relations, the undertaker and many others.

She finally got her insurance cheque and the agent tried to console her with the thought of all the money would do.

'Oh,' she sighed, 'I've had so much trouble with everything there are times when I wish Liam never fell under the bus.'

The greyhound had been a disaster at the track and the two owners were disgusted.

'Throw him in the canal,' said one.

'Don't waste time,' said the other, 'we'll just run away from him.'

A dentist of skill named Pat Boyle,
Made his fortune one day in Baldoyle.
    While drilling a tooth
    (And this is the truth)
A gusher upsurged. He'd struck oil!

There are still parts of Ireland where the train service is not as good as it should be. On one occasion a tourist complained bitterly of the slowness of the train.

'Why,' asked the harassed conductor, 'don't you get off and walk?'

'Because I'm not in that big of a hurry.'

The golf course was haunted by a malicious leprechaun who exploited the desperate ambitions of the poorer players. He slipped up beside one unfortunate man who was ploughing the fairway in a club competition.

'Look,' he said, 'if you agree never to court a woman, flirt with a girl or marry I'll help you win.'

'Done,' shouted the young golfer with the desperate abandon of his breed.

When the golfer was in the clubhouse changing and receiving the congratulations of the members the leprechaun popped up on the shelf of the locker.

'Hey,' said the little elf, 'I have to have your name for my records. What is it?'

'Father Murphy,' grinned the golfer as he adjusted his Roman collar.

One of the strangest things about life is that the poor, who need money the most, are the very ones that never have it.—FINLEY PETER DUNNE (1867-1936).

Kate and Liam were walking along the road in the late evening.

'I'm terrible afraid, Liam,' she said.

'And what would you be afraid of at all, at all?'

'I'm afraid that you might be going to kiss me.'

'And how could I kiss you and me carrying two buckets and a hen under each arm.'

'I was afraid that you might put a hen under each bucket and then kiss me.'

She came dashing into the shop in a great hurry.

'Get me a rat trap as fast as you can. I have to catch a bus.'

'Here it is, woman, but you'll never do it with this.'

The tourist lamented, 'It grieves,
That no part of my story deceives,
    In Ireland you see,
    They serve shamrock tea,
Some water well boiled with three leaves.'

A worried defendant once asked an Irish judge what was the maximum penalty for bigamy.

'Two mothers-in-law,' was the suave reply.

'How is your son the doctor doing in Dublin, Mrs Lenihan?' asked the curious neighbour.

'Grand, to tell you the living truth. He's making so much money that he doesn't have to operate on every patient now.'

A plumber in sweet Donabate,
After marriage set off feeling great.
    He got to Brighton alone,
    And emitted a groan.
He'd completely forgotten his mate.

There is a traditional Irish joke in which the natives always get the better of some boasting American. A typical story concerns the New Yorker who told Paddy of the high buildings in his native city.

'That's nothing,' said Paddy. 'At home I dropped a hammer from a scaffold one Saturday evening and it hit me on the head when I was going in on the Monday.'

SATURDAY

They asked Mick to break it to the family that their son Thady had suffered an accident.

Mick knocked on the door and the woman of the house came out.

'I'm sorry, Mam,' he said, 'to tell you that your son's gold watch is after having a bad accident.'

'What do you mean?' asked the woman. 'My son hasn't got a gold watch.'

'That's a bit of luck then,' Mick went on, 'because ten ton of rock is after falling on him.'

The visitor complained of the long muddy avenue to the hotel.

'Well now,' soothed the proprietor, 'if it was any shorter it wouldn't reach the house.'

The topers of merry Dunleer,
See more than pink rats, people fear.
    Green rabbits, blue bats,
    And six-legged cats,
Leap out of their Guinness and beer.

Ireland is covered with the remnants of monastic settlements and the islands of her shores are dotted with similar remains. Two hermits lived on adjoining islands and after twenty years one of them got lonely and called on the other. After they had a ten minute chat and Hermit B told Hermit A the latest news they parted.

Fifteen years later Hermit B got the itch for more conversation and he went over to his neighbour again.

As he entered the other's cell Hermit A turned pleasantly and asked: 'Forget something?'

A loving Co. Meath mother wrote to her son who had joined the British Army: 'Well, Dermot, I hope you get up early and don't keep the other soldiers waiting for you to come down to breakfast.'

A happy young colleen from Derry,
On ale was loving and merry,
    She dallied with sin,
    On vodka and gin,
But was rigid and frigid on sherry.

The mustard plaster is a remedy that has never been popular in Ireland. The fact that it is considered to be an English treatment may have something to do with it. In any event Mrs Carey was recommended to try it by a returned exile. When they met again an enquiry was inevitable.

'Well, Mrs Carey. Did you try the mustard plaster on your husband?'

'Indeed I did, but he wouldn't have it, Even when I made it into sandwiches he wouldn't eat it.'

The old farmer was getting ready for bed in his hotel when a lovely young girl in a see-through negligee bounced in.

'Pardon me,' she said with confusion, 'I've come to the wrong room.'

'Not alone that,' the farmer sighed. 'You're twenty years late.'

The police department magazine in Dayton, Ohio, once carried the following advertisement: *For sale, second-hand tombstone. Excellent buy for someone named Murphy.*

The innocent old lady had a huge bottle with her as she passed through the Irish Customs.

'What have you there?' asked the Customs man with suspicion.

' 'Tis Lourdes water, I'm bringing home with me.'

He took the bottle, tried some and spluttered.

'Let me tell you,' he said, 'that's not Lourdes water. That's first-class French brandy.'

'Lord bless us,' she said. 'It's a miracle!'

From poverty his business instincts had enabled him to become one of the wealthiest men in Ireland. When he arrived at a Galway hotel in the middle of a blazing June day the manager was a little confused to see the skis, snowshoes, toboggans and winter sports equipment that was brought in.

'Pardon me, sir,' he apologised, 'but you must know we have no snow in Galway at this time of the year.'

The tycoon waved his hand.

'Don't you be bothering about it,' he said, 'I'm having the snow sent on with my heavy baggage.'

> The fairy banshee moans and moans,
> For she's known for her musical groans,
>   She wails in B sharp,
>   Like a dyspeptic harp,
> Winning prizes for anguished octones.

The Boston taxi driver backed into the stationary fruit stall and in a second he had a cop beside him.

'Name?'

'Brendan O'Connor.'

'Same as mine. Where are you from?'

'Co. Leitrim.'

'Same as me. . . .'

The policeman paused with his pen in the air.

'Hold on a moment and I'll come back and talk about the old county. I want to say something to this fella that ran into the back of your cab.'

'That's the world's worst dog,' complained Clancy as he pointed to his howling dog.

'Ah,' said his friend Flavin, 'maybe the dog is in pain.'

'Pain, is it? He's sitting on a thistle and he's too lazy to get up.'

An Irish political prisoner escaped from jail by digging a tunnel that emerged in a school playground. As he emerged to the open air he couldn't help shouting at a small girl, 'I'm free . . . I'm free.'

'That's nothing,' she said scornfully; 'I'm four.'

Said the Druid to St. Pat, 'It's a fake,
That thing that you chase ain't a snake.'
    But the thing's vicious bite,
    Made him cry, 'You are right,
Get me 'asp'–irin fast for my ache.'

Murphy had served in the Irish Navy and then, anxious to see the world, he switched over to the United States fleet. From the start he was glum and when they visited Japan he was glummer. Finally his commanding officer sent for him.

'Murphy, you seem unhappy. You have the best conditions possible; you're seeing the world so what can we do to make you cheer up?'

'Please, sir, could you let me cycle home to Clones at weekends.'

On one occasion it was proposed in New York that a gondola should be introduced to Central Park. An Irish councillor supported the idea with enthusiasm.

'Let's get two gondolas,' he said, 'A male and a female.'

A sadistic wife of Glasthule,
In oil boiled her husband. 'Twas cruel.
    She said, 'In my car,
    This mix will go far,
For he'll be of some use. The old fuel!'

They were completely drunk but when they saw the black crepe on the door they decided to go in and show respect for the dead.

They tiptoed into a darkened room lit only by two candles on a grand piano. Heads down, they went over and knelt beside it, said a prayer and tiptoed out again.

As they staggered away Aongus shook his head at Fergus.

'I'll tell you one thing, Fergus. . . .'

'Whash that?'

'That corpse had the finest set of teeth I ever saw.'

Moore Street in Dublin is famous for its street dealers, most of whom have tongues that would file stainless steel.

'I want to complain about the bananas you sold me yesterday. They were awful' hard to skin.'

The dealer drew herself up.

'Look, mam, what do you want at the price? Zip fasteners?'

Look lively,' shouted the sergeant to the cook; 'You'll have to make dinner for twenty more soldiers who've arrived in camp.'

The cook turned to his assistant.

'Ultan,' he called, 'throw two more buckets of water in the Irish stew.'

It hadn't been a good harvest and they didn't want each other to forget it.

'Flannery, I'm telling you the wheat was so poor I had to harvest it with scissors.'

'That's nothing, O'Grady. I had to lather my field and shave it.'

'I think, Murragh,' she said, 'I'll bring home a bottle of sea water for my rheumatism.'

'Do if you want to, but don't fill the bottle.'

'Why?'

'You oul' amadan, sure don't you know you have to leave room for the tide?'

When asked to a fancy dress ball,
An odd bod who lived in Glenstal,
　　Dressed up as a tree,
　　Now all dogs agree,
He'd never have pleased as a wall.

Many English students come to Trinity College in Dublin and on one occasion a harassed professor was interviewing one of them.

'And, Basset-Claghorne, do you know anything about ethics?'

'No, thir, I'm from Thuththex.'

A classical Belfast joke tells of a new policeman who found a dead horse in Chichester Street, Belfast.

'How do you spell Chichester?' he asked some of the people around him but no one knew.

'All right, then. Give me a wee hand to pull the animal into Mary Street.'

A lady who lived in Newbliss,
Would stand on her head for a kiss,
When people asked why,
She replied, cute and sly,
'Men go to my head when like this.'

Ferguson the blacksmith came in with a badly-damaged foot. The doctor was surprised, for Ferguson was a careful man.

'What happened to you, Paudeen?' he asked.

'Well, thirty-three years ago I was a young apprentice with Twomey of Ballinanaspickbuidhe . . .'

'But about your foot . . .?'

'This is about me foot. Twomey had a daughter and your eyes could gaze on her like the way a bullock would eat good grass. The first night I was there she came in when I was in bed and asked if I was comfortable and if I wanted anything and I said I didn't. The next night she came in when I was in bed and she wearing her nightdress and she asked me if there was any single thing she could get me or do for me and I told her I was as comfortable as a bug in a rug. The next night she came in and the girl hadn't a thing on her and she asked me if she could do anything for me and not wanting to keep her standing in the cold and she without a shift I said there was nothing.'

'What has that got to do with your foot, Ferguson?' asked the doctor impatiently.

'Sure it was only this morning that I finally thought of what she meant and I was so annoyed with meself that I threw me ten-pound hammer against the wall and it rebounded and broke me ankle.'

To quote Sir Boyle Roche: 'Happy are the parents that have no children.'

> A lady they called her in Trim,
> Though her right to the title was slim,
>   And doubts started to mount,
>   With her chromosome count.
> Was she 'her' or an 'it' or a 'him'?

Mrs O'Growney was puzzled.

'Why,' she asked her friend Mrs Twomey, 'are the O'Connors learning French?'

'Don't you know? They've adopted a French baby and they want to be able to understand it when it starts talking.'

On the rough trip to the Aran Islands the tourist lay over the rail and suffered.

'Cheer up, mo cairde,' said a member of the crew, 'sure no one ever died of sea sickness yet.'

'Ah, sure,' gasped the victim, 'isn't it the hope of dying that keeps me alive.'

Father Burke looked over the class and then asked Sean: 'Do you say a prayer before meals in your house?'

'We don't have to, Father. Me mother is a good cook.'

The little boy had been sitting close to the confession box door for a long time before Father Casey noticed him.

'Have you been listening to confessions all evening?' thundered the priest.

'Oh, no, Father. I'm only here since the woman who slept with the sailor came out.'

'And why, Johnny, do you think your daddy is kind to animals?'

'Well he told us, teacher, that he'd like to kill the man who scratches horses.'

An ancient old man of Dun Laoghaire,
Said, 'Of pleasure and joy I've grown waoghaire . . .
  The life that is pure,
  Will suit me I'm sure,
It's healthy and noble though draoghaire.'

It hadn't been much of a crash, but Finnegan emerged completely paralysed in spite of the suspicion of the insurance agent. When finally the jury awarded a huge sum in damages the agent spoke firmly to Finnegan.

'You got the money but I'll watch you like a hawk from now on and if you move I'll sue you for the lot.'

Solemn faced, Finnegan whispered back.

'You'd better come with me to Lourdes then for the miracle.'

He walked into Flavin's Bar and asked for a glass of water. He drank it and walked out. The next day he was in again and he asked for a glass of water, drank it and was getting ready to go.

'Here,' complained the barman, 'you come in here, ask for a glass of water; drink it and then walk out . . .'

'What do you want me to do . . . stagger?'

> Cosmetically Lil of Kilquade,
> Had beauty that ne'er seemed to fade,
> When tanned by the sun,
> She looked twenty-one,
> But she seemed fifty-six in the shade.

He was a terrible wreck and his trembling hands told the whole story.

'Tell me,' asked his doctor, 'do you drink much?'

'Deed I don't. Sure I spill most of it.'

When George Moore, the Irish author, was eighty, he was asked how he had managed to have such a long life. 'I believe,' said Moore, 'that it is due to the fact that I never smoked, drank or touched a girl—until I was ten years of age.'

Murray was muttering to himself with fiendish glee when his friend Hyland asked him what it was all about.

'I'll tell you, Hyland. That amadan O'Rourke keeps slapping me on the back. Well, I've put a stick of dynamite under my coat and this time he'll blow his arm off.'

A nervous six-footer named Bridget,
Would wriggle and squirm, twitch and fidget,
    But she knew perfect peace,
    And a psychic release,
When she found true romance with a midget.

At one period of the eighteenth century there was an Irish hangman in London. On one occasion he was given an expensive present by the condemned man just before the execution.

'Long life to your honour,' he cried delightedly as he pulled the bolt.

The American tourist had been complaining a great deal about the food.

'Here,' he said to the waitress holding out a piece of meat for inspection, 'do you call that pig?'

'Which end of the fork, sir?' she asked sweetly.

'Heat,' explained Rafferty to his friend Mulligan, 'makes things expand and cold makes them contract.'

Mulligan laughed with a sneer.

"Tis mad you are entirely. Mad,' he said. 'Who ever heard the like of that.'

'Well,' replied Rafferty, 'how do you account for the longer days in summer and the short ones in the winter?'

A driver whose breath would burst a breathalyser drove his car right into an old cottage on the Cork Road. As he drew up neatly beside the fireplace he leaned out and questioned the old lady sitting in the armchair.

'Shay, ish this the road to Dublin?'

Timidly she shook her head.

'No, sir, you'll have to turn right over there by the piano and keep straight on when you pass the scullery table.'

Cried a pious young fella Pat Geoghan,
  'I'm in love with a sinuous pagan,
    Her legs are just fine,
    But she cannot be mine,
  'Til Golden Calves all, are forsaken.'

The drunk staggered into his car and fumbled with the keys while a big Civic Guard—an Irish policeman—stared across at him. Finally he went over and spoke to the driver.

'You're not seriously thinking of driving that car the way you are.'

'Look, oul son, I'm in no fit condition to walk.'

O'Hara fell from the scaffold and dropped two storeys. They gathered around him and the foreman asked: 'Did the fall hurt you, Peadar?'

The victim felt his aching bones.

'It wasn't the fall hurt me. T'was the sudden stop.'

A neurotic in old Ballindine,
  Lay down on a railway line,
    But it was such a bore,
    For the four-forty-four,
  Didn't come 'til a quarter past nine.

The farmer was giving his last instructions to the lawyer.

'. . . and put Paddy down for £2,000. Put Shane down for £3,000 and see that another £3,000 goes to Liam. . .'

'Just a moment, Mr Carey,' whispered the puzzled lawyer, 'where is all this money to come from?'

'To hell with them,' muttered Carey, 'let them work for it the way I had to . . .'

Doctors in Roscommon are busy men and he was a little absent-minded as he sat down to breakfast. His wife put her hands over his eyes and when he opened them there was a new pen in front of him.

'For our wedding anniversary, Padraig,' she smiled.

'Well thanks,' he said with embarrassment, 'and when it's yours I must give you something.'

Said Murphy to Quinn: 'Did you hear about Mickey? He fell thirty feet into a Guinness vat and broke his pledge.'

'My girl friend,' cried love-worn Flann,
'Will make a good cook for a man.'
'I will,' she agreed,
'Give him a fine feed,
But jam I can't make, though I can.'

The two mercenary soldiers were trudging through a nasty patch of jungle.
'And you tell me, Murphy, you joined up because of a girl in Ireland. Why don't you forget her?'
'Forget her? How can I forget a girl with a name like Gobnait ni Mhathghamhna?'

Aunt Mary was paying her nephew's university fees and she was pleased to see how hard he was concentrating on his language lessons.

'He tells me,' she announced proudly, 'that he needs ten pounds for French, twelve pounds for Italian, thirty pounds for Scotch and ninety-five pounds for pure Irish.'

Mrs Hennessy was out driving and for the first time she noticed linesmen working up on telegraph poles.

'What are they doing up there?' she asked her husband.

'Nothing,' he said. 'They heard you were coming.'

Miss Balfour, the daughter of the Chief Secretary for Ireland in the dreadful famine of 1847, told one grim story of her experience in giving out relief.

One poor victim assured her, 'Oh Miss, only for the famine we'd be starving altogether.'

The doctor decided to put Mrs Mulligan on a diet.

'You can have three lettuce leaves,' he said, 'one piece of dry toast, a glass of orange juice and a tomato.'

'Very well, doctor,' said Mrs Mulligan meekly. 'Do I take them before or after meals?'

There was a young fellow named Peadar,
Who seemed to grow madder and madder,
    He ate nothing but glue,
    And was stuck through and through,
Which made him much saner but sadder.

The bride of the champion runner was about to boil an egg and felt confused.

'John, dear,' she pleaded, 'will you go out and run a mile so that I can time the eggs?'

They were watching the new man set out from the Dublin Street Sweeping Department.

'He's not doing bad,' said O'Keefe sagely. 'I think he'll learn the trade.'

'Don't be mad,' growled Keating scornfully, 'he's only doing up and down sweeping. Wait until he has to do a bit of fancy work around a lamp post.'

The Behans won a large prize in a competition and bought a big house in the country.

Mrs Behan was showing off the estate to a poor relative from the city when they came to the poultry farm.

'Mrs Behan,' asked the visitor, 'do your hens lay eggs?'

'I suppose they do,' said Mrs Behan haughtily, 'but they don't have to. We can afford to buy them now.'

Then there was the keeper at the level crossing in Co. Kilkenny who kept the gates half open because he was half expecting a train.

Phelan was burying his third wife but O'Donnell, his neighbour on the next farm, wouldn't go to the funeral.

'And why won't you?' asked Mrs O'Donnell impatiently.

'Well, to tell you the truth I feel ashamed. He's asked me so often, and I've never asked him back once.'

He was an old-fashioned Irish doctor and she was a very modern mother.

'Crying, is it?' said the doctor. 'Well, when everything else fails just put your finger in his mouth.'

'But, doctor,' she said with horrified expression, 'is that hygienic . . .?'

'In your case,' he said smoothly, 'I think you should boil it first . . .'

A lovely girl swimmer named Sive,
Was swingy, tough, eager, alive.
'I keep my head above water,'
She said, 'as I oughter,
But I like best of all a low dive.'

Coming from a linen mill one girl spoke to another:
'For dear sake, Sar' Jane, will ye just look at her. If she'd another
wave in her head she'd capsize.'

The Belfast sales manager had a busy week in the country and on
Saturday evening he was exhausted when he dropped into the
local bar to have a quick one before going home.

'Give me something to pick me up,' he asked.

'Brandy? Vodka? Tullamore Dew? Bushmills?'

'No, no. I need something different.'

'Well,' said the barman with hesitation, 'the only thing that
might do it would be our parish priest's special.'

'I'll try it,' said the sales manager and he had to admit that the
first made him feel a new man while the second and third sent
him home floating on air.

He was telling a friend about it, 'It was terrific,' he said, 'and
the next morning I jumped out of bed and gave all the family
their breakfasts, packed them into the car and took them to an
early Mass. It was when we came out that the trouble started.'

'In what way?' asked his friend.

'Sure we're not Roman Catholics. We're Presbyterians.'

'Mr Corrigan, I'd like to have a day off to attend my mother-in-law's funeral.'

'So would I, Flynn, but she's an absolute picture of health.'

The English buyer looked dubiously at the steeplechaser offered to him.

'Are you sure it's a good jumper?' he asked.

'Good jumper, is it . . . why, we have to give notice to air traffic control when he's running.'

'My people,' boasted McCourt, 'can trace their ancestors back to the Kings of Tara.'

'I suppose they were in the Ark with Noah as well.'

'Not at all. They had their own boat.'

On the road to Cornamona, Finnegan was shocked to see a cow on the back seat of a farmer's car with a large piece of bread on its head.

At the next crossroads he pulled in beside the other man's car and, lowering the window, he called out.

'Look,' he said, 'do you know you have a cow on the back seat with a big piece of bread on top of its head?'

'I do,' said the farmer furiously. 'And it's none of your business, me man, what I put in my sandwiches.'

The missioner was warning his congregation about the dangers of drinking.

'If you put a worm in water,' he said, 'it will stay vigorous and healthy, but if you put a worm in Irish whiskey it dies.'

A few days later he met O'Guaille in the village street and asked him if he had been impressed with the sermon on drink.

'Indeed I was, Father,' said O'Guaille, 'and I was terrible interested to know that if you drink Irish whiskey you won't suffer from worms.'

The farm labourer had a bad rash that the village doctor had never seen before. He looked up his medical books but couldn't find anything like it. He went back and examined the patient again but without any luck. Then he had an inspiration.

'Tell me,' he asked, 'have you ever had this rash before?'

'I have that,' said the man.

'Ah,' diagnosed the doctor with shrewd professionalism, 'you have it again so.'

While hunting around Ballybay,
Pretty Ellen gave no man his way.
   Though pressed hard to yield,
   Trotting over a field,
Her horse answered for her, 'Neigh! Neigh!'

Fagan made a lot of money in his furniture store one year so he went to Paris for a holiday.

'Twas grand,' he told his friends in Galway.

'How did you get on,' asked McGiolla Padraig, 'and you with not a word of the language at you.'

'Twas simple. Look at the girleen I met in the park. I drew a picture of a taxi and she knew what I meant so we went for a drive. I drew a lot of plates and cutlery and she knew I wanted her to go for dinner. I drew two people dancing and we went to a night club. At the end of the evening she took the pencil from me and drew a big double bed . . .'

'Would you believe it,' said McGiolla Padraig with awe. 'She even knew you were in the furniture business.'

The farmer's wife told Brigid, the family servant, that five shillings would be deducted from her wages if the family had to cook their breakfast themselves. A few mornings later Brigid staggered down long after the day had started.

'Brigid, we had to get our own breakfast again.'

'Well, sure amn't I payin' you for it?'

It was three o'clock in the morning when the telephone rang beside the bed of O'Gorman, the publican.

'Mr O'Gorman,' said the alcohol-saturated voice of Cleary, 'what time do you open in the morning?'

'Ten o'clock, Cleary,' snapped O'Gorman and hung up.

At seven o'clock the phone rang and it was Cleary again, 'Whash time dush you open?'

'Ten o'clock but you're not going to be let in.'

'I'sh don't want to get in. I want to gesh out . . .'

Grudgingly the small farmer installed electric light for his wife when he found she was pregnant. On the night of the delivery he waited outside the bedroom.

'You have a son,' the doctor called out.

'And another!'

'And a girl!'

Madly the farmer pulled out the fuses and plunged the house into darkness.

'What's up?' cried the doctor.

'Sure I had to do something. I think it must have been the light that was attracting them.'

'And have you made your will, Shamuseen?'

'Indeed I have. All of me fortune goes to the doctor that saves my life.'

> A coy maiden of Glenmalure,
> Had a mind that was perfectly pure.
>   She fainted away,
>   In a delicate way,
> If anyone spoke of manure.

'Is that 999?' Sweeney asked urgently.

'You have the wrong number. This is 998.'

'Well, could you go in to the people next door and tell them to send an ambulance? There's been an accident.'

Casey was slightly drunk and he wandered around losing money everywhere. He finally staggered up to a machine, put in a shilling and, pressing a lever, got a sandwich. He put in another and got another. He was holding eighteen of them when the proprietor came up.

'Look,' he said, 'don't you think you have enough of those?'

'Give up now, is it,' said Murphy, 'just when I'm winning?'

The Irish army platoon got lost on manoeuvres in Kerry. The sergeant called out to a passing local, 'How much further to Dingle?'

'Two miles,' was the reply.

They marched on and after an hour the sergeant asked another man how far they had to go to Dingle.

'Two miles,' came the answer.

'After another hour they asked again and the reply this time was still, 'Two miles.'

For a moment the sergeant looked depressed. Then, wiping the perspiration from his face, he straightened his back.

'Come on, men,' he ordered, 'at least we're holding our own.'

Guard Sweeney woke up with an awful headache after a night of testing bottles for illegal spirits. He rang the police station and explained to the sergeant that he was too ill to report for duty.

'That's all right, Sweeney,' said the sergeant soothingly, 'go back to bed and look after yourself.'

He hung up the phone.

'You were very soft with him, Sergeant,' said his assistant.

'Was I then? Wait 'til he finds out that this was his day off.'

Kennedy came along the road to find his friend Finnegan lying in the ditch where the playful impact of a ten ton lorry had landed him. As he lay on his back groaning and moaning the rain came pouring down and the lightning flashed about him.

'Kennedy—Kennedy—get me a rabbi. Get me a rabbi.'

'Are you mad, Finnegan? Sure you're a Roman Catholic and what would you want a rabbi for?'

The victim opened his eyes reproachfully: 'Arrah, Kennedy you wouldn't think of asking a priest to come out on a night like that.'

The somnambulant people of Bangor,
Are known for their softness and languor.
    They sleep very late,
    You can't rouse them at eight,
And never at all into anger.

Mrs Moriarty was buying medicine for her husband and a preparation for the sick horse.

'Be careful,' said the chemist, 'that you don't get the bottles mixed.'

'Oh, you can be sure of it,' she said with emphasis. 'Sure wouldn't it be awful if anything happened to the poor animal before the spring ploughing?'

The Protestant minister was impressed when he was shown over Father Quinn's new residence.

'You know,' he said, 'this is far better than what my wife and I have at the parsonage.'

'That's logical,' said Father Quinn. 'Protestant ministers have better halves and Catholic priests have better quarters.'

Finnegan's phone rang in the small hours of the morning and it was Hourihan who wanted to know the time.

' 'Tis four o'clock in the morning.'

'Thanks,' said Hourihan, 'I hope I didn't disturb you.'

'Not a bit of it. Sure I had to get up to answer this phone anyways.'

If a female duck is a duchess
Would a female spook be a spuchess.
If a number of cows are cattle
Would a number of bows be a battle.
If drinking too hard makes a drunkard
Would thinking too hard make a thunkard.
If a chap in New York is a New Yorker
Would a chappie from Cork be a corker.

They hadn't met for a long time.

'How have you been, Kinsella?' asked Fagan.

'Deed I wasn't too well. For a long time I thought I was a sick Irish wolfhound and I had a stew of psychiatrists about me.'

'You recovered, I hope?'

'Indeed I did. Feel my nose.'

An old man of fair Ballinlough,
Made black pudding of chocolate and rock,
    Manure and old rope,
    Prussic acid and soap,
Wrapped up in an old army sock.

The Irishman was late back to the building site after lunch.

'Where have you been?' the foreman asked. 'You're an hour late.'

'I was only getting my hair cut.'

'Well, you shouldn't do it in the company's time.'

'It grew in the company's time.'

'It didn't all grow in the company's time,' the foreman answered.

'Well, I didn't get it all cut.'

The difference between the three Celtic races is that the Scot keeps the Sabbath and everything he can lay hands on; the Welshman prays on his knees on Sunday and everyone else the rest of the week; while the Irishman doesn't know what he wants but will fight to the death for it.

'Shamus, you're using your knife to eat. Why don't you use the fork.'

'Ah, Mrs Mooney, it leaks.'

Father O'Leary had given a long sermon to his congregation and he was apologising to Mick Cafferkey.

'Don't apologise at all, Father,' said Mick with a grin. 'Sure you've done a lot to shorten the winter.'

Father Scally stopped Owen on his way into the church.

'Owen, could you come back tomorro'w night for confession? We have hundreds in the church at the moment. You haven't committed a murder since the last time?

'Indeed I haven't, Father. I'll come back tomorrow night.'

On his way out he met Declan.

'Go home, Declan, and come back tomorrow. They're only hearing the murderers tonight.'

Mary Murphy had drunk with a sheikh,
For what seemed the best part of a weikh.
   Gurgling, 'I'm full, I think,
    To the edge of my brink,
If I take any more why I'll leikh.'

He bent down to switch channels on the TV set when a sharp pain hit him in the back.

'I think,' he groaned, 'I'm getting lumbago.'

'Turn it off so,' his wife urged. 'Sure we wouldn't understand a word they say.'

The boss wanted to test Patrick's judgment.

'Tell me, Pat,' he asked, 'what would you do with two thousand pounds?'

Pat raised his eyebrows.

'Heavens above, I wouldn't know. Sure I hadn't a notion you were going to pay me that much.'

The psychiatrist was very pleased with Shaun's progress.

'You're doing fine, Shaun,' he said soothingly. 'You've improved much more than Barry. He's going around telling everyone he wants to buy the Bank of Ireland.'

Shaun suddenly grew very excited.

'Oh, the ruffian,' he shouted. 'I've told him a dozen times I won't sell.'

She went to the Birmingham Railway station on coming back from Ireland.

'I want a ticket for Orla,' she said.

The clerk searched his lists but was completely baffled.

'Madam,' he said, 'where's Orla?'

'Over there,' she answered innocently, 'sucking peppermints she is.'

The doctor told Fursa O'Siochain, a newly wealthy businessman, that he'd need a slight operation.

'Would you like a local anaesthetic?' he asked.

'Hang the expense,' cried Fursa. 'Get the best. Use imported.'

> The things that occur on the shingle,
> Of the beaches surrounding old Dingle,
>   Can only be said,
>   In the bed of the wed,
> For they'd tingle the single to mingle.

'Mary, we've been courtin' in this field for the past seven years.'

'We have, Shaun.'

'We won't be doin' it for long more.'

'And why, Shaun?'

'They're buildin' houses in it.'

With two ingots of lead, one under each arm, Conor came down the gangplank of the cargo ship. Suddenly he slipped and fell into the water.

As he came up for the first time he called out for a rope. Then he went down and came up again.

'Throw me a rope in the name of the seven saints of Aran,' he yelled, and then went down once more.

He was about to sink once more when he made a final plea.

'If yiz don't throw me a rope I'll let go the lead.'

'Doctor,' Kinsella said, 'my family is worried about my taste in Aran sweaters.'

'There's no harm in that,' the doctor said with surprise. 'I like a good Aran sweater myself.'

'Ah,' said Kinsella, 'but is it with or without tomato sauce?'

The nervous tourist didn't like standing too near the fantastic giant wall of Co. Clare's Cliffs of Moher.

'What would I do,' he said to the guide, 'if I fell over.'

'Look to the right in that case,' enthused the eager conductor. 'You'd love the view.'

Mrs O'Casey was proud of her newly-acquired wealth and let everyone know of the advantages it gave her.

'Of course,' she told her friend Mrs Donnelly, 'I always clean my diamonds with ammonia, and I find soap suds best for my emeralds. What do you use?'

Mrs Donnelly shrugged her shoulders. 'To tell you the truth, as soon as mine get dirty I throw them away.'

A landlady mean in Ardee,
Served little of honey at tea.
A new lodger said,
As he shook a sad head,
'I'm glad, Mam, to see you've one bee.'

'Are you getting rid of the incubator, Higgins?'
'Of course I am. I've had it six months and it hasn't laid an egg yet.'

'What's wrong with you, Mullarkey?' asked the doctor.
'Two years ago, doctor, I swallowed two ten shilling pieces, and I want you to do something about them.'
'Heavens, man, why didn't you come to me two years ago?'
'Sure, doctor, I didn't need the money until now.'

'Did you hear that Slattery has invented an invisible deodorant?'
'No, and what good is it?'
'Well, if you use it you vanish and no one knows where the smell's coming from.'

Sir John Mahaffy, the Irish wit, said that an Irish atheist was a man who went about wishing to God he could believe in God.

The hotel owner was disturbed by the length of time it had taken his new maid to do the simple job.
'Mary,' he shouted down to the kitchen, 'have you filled the salt cellars yet?'
'Deed I haven't, sir,' she called back fretfully. 'The holes are so small it's awful hard to get the stuff in.'

There was a young laddie of Louth,
Who returned from a trip to the south,
  His father asked did he
  See anything of Sidney,
But the answer was, 'No, he was outh.'

The Judge was stern.

'O'Driscoll,' he rapped, 'have you ever been up before me?'

'I don't know, Judge. What time do you usually get up at?'

'Listen to all the booing,' said the Abbey playwright's friend on the first night of the new play.

'There's some clapping,' said the author with optimism.

'Don't fool yourself. That's for the booing.'

A foreign prince bought Ballinahinch Castle in Connemara and was treated with great respect by the locals except on one occasion. He was fishing on the local lake with a gillie when he hooked a big trout.

'Haul him in, your Highness!' cried the gillie. 'Play him, your Lordship! Watch out, your nobility! He's breaking away sir...he's gone...you stupid foreign heathen!'

He was a small farmer who had managed to live for many years on ten acres and faith in the Lord. Now he was preparing to pass on to Green Pastures. He could hear the family whispering about the funeral arrangements.

'Will we have two cars with the hearse?'

'Sure what do we want them for? The pony and cart will do.

'Maybe we should get a few wreaths?'

'Waste of money. We'll do without.'

He struggled and sat up.

'Bring me my trousers, let ye. I'll walk to the graveyard and ye can cut out the hearse.'

The Birmingham landlady wanted to please her Irish lodger and the first day she gave him two slices of bread for his package lunch. He didn't seem satisfied so she gave him four slices the next day and then six slices and had to go on until he was getting ten. Even this wasn't enough so, in despair, she cut the loaf in half and put ham between the pieces. When he came in that evening she asked: 'Had you enough today, Colum?'

'It wasn't bad,' he said grudgingly, 'but I see you're back to the two slices again.'

> An ambitious girl in Kilskyre,
> Used paraffin lighting a fire.
> She soared into the sky,
> Without even 'Good-bye,'
> Now her place in the world is much higher.

Mrs Mulligan was in the witness box. The prosecution counsel indicated her husband.

'Do you mean to say that a physical wreck like your husband could give you a black eye?'

'He wasn't a physical wreck when he gave it to me.'

The Roman Catholic parish priest of a Belfast church was amazed to find two bigoted and drunken Orange Protestants outside his window at two o'clock in the morning.

'What do you want?' he called.

'Well, we wanted ye to tell us if it was tha Pope that called the Ecumenical council?'

'Look, come back in the morning and I'll discuss it when you're sober.'

'Sure when we're sober, we don't give a damn about the Pope.'

In the magazine *Blarney* published in the last century a ruffian was defined as a man who would sharpen a knife on his father's tombstone to cut his mother's throat.

A meek little country man came to town and visited the local health office. He explained the problem.

'We all live in one room out in Newtownmoneenluggagh. Meself and six brothers. One of 'em keeps three greyhounds in with him and Tadgh has his mountain goat with the weak chest that can't go out in the field and Colman keeps his wolfhound in the room so that we have to let Padraig have his five budgies. Of course, Francis only has his goldfish so they don't matter. But the air is terrible and the smell is shocking.'

The Health Officer was sympathetic but saw no difficulty.

'Surely it would be easy to open a window and let in some air.'

'Open the window, he says! Sure what about my fifteen pigeons?'

Peadar woke up in a hospital bed and he knew that he was suffering from more than the normal hangover. Groaning with pain, he turned over to find his faithful friend Terence beside the bed.

'What happened to me, Terence?'

'You went up on the roof of "The Silver Swan" and bet you could jump off and fly over the city.'

'Why didn't you stop me?' groaned Peadar.

'Sure I had a ten bob bet on you.'

A girl from Belfast name of Alice,
Drew rude things on the Vatican Palace.
 She said, 'Now this deed,
 Comes from aesthetic need,
And not from a Protestant malice.'

A story which has gone the rounds for the past hundred years or so is a classic Irish joke which must be repeated. Two men were waiting for the local landlord to pass by so that they could ventilate his hide with buckshot. He was a long time in coming and an awful thought occurred to Mick.

'Paddy,' he said, 'say a prayer that nothing's happened to the poor man.'

His cigar, his suit and everything about him proclaimed prosperity as he entered a bar in a small town in County Mayo.

'Well, well,' he said, 'fifteen years ago I left and all I had was five shillings that John Conroy loaned me. Ah, I suppose that poor John has passed on by now and how I wish I could meet him . . .'

'Here I am . . . here I am. I'm still living here,' said John eagerly as he pushed his way forward.

'I'm glad to see you, John, and I was going to ask if you wouldn't mind lending me fifteen bob to make it the even pound I owe you.'

Seanin came running into the barn to his brother shouting: 'Quick, get the shovels. The Da is after falling into the manure pit up to his bootlaces.'

'Sure can't he walk out so?' asked Cormack.

' 'Deed he can't. He fell in head first.'

He was the greatest drinker the village had ever known.

'Jimin,' asked his wife, 'are you particular where we bury you?'

'If it's all the same to you, Brid, just pour me back into the barrel.'

The little car behind Bartley's lorry crashed into him as he turned right.

'Here,' said the driver of the small car, 'why didn't you put your hand out?'

'Put me hand out, is it?' Bartley said indignantly. 'If you couldn't see the lorry how could you see my hand?'

Cried a silly old girl name of Maeve,
Digging holes in the floor of a caeve,
   'Australia's my aim,
   Tho' the work is a shame,
But expenses and fares I will saeve.'

Murphy told Quinn that his wife is driving him to drink.
Quinn thinks he's lucky because his own wife makes him walk.

An Irish magician made a feature of sawing a woman in half. After his retirement a friend asked him what had happened to his assistant.

'She's living now in Belfast and Dublin,' he answered.

The new maid was from Ireland and Mrs Fanshawe-Edderington wanted to make sure she knew the rules of the household.

'Kathleen,' she advised, 'we have breakfast sharp at eight each morning.'

Kathleen gave an expansive nod.

'Good, m'am,' she nodded, 'and if I'm not up just go ahead without me.'

The chemist was most polite to the new president of Ballynacaoire when she selected soap.

'Madam,' he asked, 'do you want it scented or unscented?'

'I'll take it with me, sir,' she said, 'if you don't mind.'

The Bishop received a large number of complaints about Father O'Reilly's bitter attacks on the British from his London pulpit.

'You can't go on speaking to your congregation in that fashion,' His Lordship told the priest. 'Remember the law of charity and the fact that you live in the country of which you speak so harshly. Next week I ask you to give a sermon on the Last Supper. With that topic you will not be able to indulge your bias.'

Father O'Reilly accepted the rebuke mildly, but the Bishop discreetly attended the service the following Sunday to check that all went well. He had no cause to complain and not once in the course of his sermon did the priest refer to the Base, Brutal and Bloody Saxon. The Bishop noticed with satisfaction that he was drawing to the end of what had been a very good and inoffensive piece of religious instruction.

'. . . and having asked all the disciples, it was time to turn to Judas,' Father O'Reilly said. ' "Judas," came the question, "wouldst thou betray me?" '

The priest paused and looked around.

'Judas looked back without blinking an eyelid, and then with the treachery of his kind he answered, "Not bloomin' likely, Guv".'

The widow of Ballinalickey,
Was married eight times and was tricky.
　　When she led without falter
　　Young Mike to the altar,
They sang 'Him' Number Nine for poor Mickey.

The Countess of Fingall caught some of the religious bitterness in Northern Ireland—now dying out—when she related in *Seventy Years Young* how a visitor admired all the churches in the area—Catholic, Presbyterian, Methodist. Plymouth Brethren, Quaker Meeting Places and the rest.

'They build them for sake of religion,' he said with admiration.

'No, they build them for spite,' answered the Countess.

'Isn't it a pity that the Maguires have no children, Mr Flynn?'

'It is indeed, but I hear that sterility is hereditary on both sides of their family.'

'Oh, Mrs Carey, my husband went out six months ago for a loaf of bread and never came back. What should I do?'

'Well, since you ask me I'd say not to wait any more. Send one of the children down for another one.'

Mr Clarke stared at the young suitor with surprise.

'You want to marry my daughter? Why, she's only a girl.'

'I know sir. That's why.'

The problem had McGillicuddy annoyed so he put a notice on his shop counter:

Mothers are asked not to put their children sitting on the bacon slicer as we are getting a little behind with the orders.

'I've been drinking whiskey all week to cure my sciatica.'

'I can give you a cure, Mr Cummisky.'

'Shut up. I don't want to hear it.'

The Irish policeman was doing his best to stop a suicide from jumping off a New York skyscraper.

'Think of your sweetheart,' he shouted at the man.

'I haven't got one,' came the reply.

'Think of your father and mother,' pleaded the cop.

'I'm an orphan,' wailed the suicide.

'Think of the saints of Ireland,' begged the Law.

'Why should I? I'm English.'

'Jump, you swine, jump!'

An Irish judge, infuriated by the noise and disturbance in the public gallery, ordered the court room to be cleared.

'All the blackguards that aren't lawyers will have to leave, he cried.

A horse-loving lady of Howth,
Said: 'I'm changing my diet so take nowth,
   I intend for a start,
   Not to dine à la carte,
But to eat with my nag table d'oat.'

Said Quinn to Burke: 'You know now it was so dry that the trees were pulling themselves up by the roots and chasing dogs. Not a word of a lie.'

On an Irish radio show for children the following dialogue is supposed to have taken place.

'And you tell me that your father's horse fell into a hole. And did your Daddy shoot the horse in the head?' asked the compere.

'Oh, no, sir. He shot the horse in the hole.'

He applied for a job but the foreman said the factory was overstaffed.

'Take me on,' pleaded Oscar, 'and I promise you won't even notice the bit I'll do.'

The Co. Cork hurler arrived at the gates of Heaven and the shadowy figure guarding the entrance had a word to say.

'Is there anything you have done that might keep you from entering Paradise?'

'Well, now you see, sir,' said the embarrassed hurler, 'I played for St. Finbarr's in Cork and in the last game I missed the ball with my stick and I kicked it into the goal and we won, see And St. Finbarr's shouldn't have got the match, see.'

'Pass within!' said the shadowy figure.

'But, St. Peter, I don't think I should.'

'I am not St. Peter. He is off duty, so pass within.'

'Well and who are you then?'

'St. Finbarr.'

Two cannibals were talking and one complained that he got an awful pain after eating an Irish Franciscan missionary.

'How did you cook him?' asked O'Oool, the chief.

'I boiled him.'

'That's the explanation,' nodded O'Oool sagely. 'You should never boil Franciscans. They're Friars.'

A young woman in church at Kildare,
Was distracted by noise while at prayer,
   The squeak of the shoes,
   And the rattle of pews,
Made her dash from her seat in despair.

It was a favourite story of Brendan Behan and it was supposed to have happened in a Dublin municipal housing scheme some years ago. One house had been the centre of various infections and the local doctor decided to call and see for himself what was wrong. The household, he noted, could be more easily ploughed than washed; they were so coated with Mother Earth.

'Do you,' he asked the woman who came to the door, 'have a bath in the house?'

'We do, doctor,' she sniffed, 'but thank God we haven't had to use it for the past ten years.'

It was a tough spot and bullets flew from all sides. The tough Irish sergeant was not going to allow his men to retreat.

'Stay here,' he shouted, 'and keep firing even if you run out of ammunition!'

The sun was setting behind the Connemara hills as the tourist pulled into the village. The utter beauty of the moment made him remark to a local: 'That is one of the loveliest sights I've seen in my tour of Ireland and that's saying something.'

The local hung his head modestly.

'Well, now,' he said, 'when you come to think of the matter, it's not a bad sunset for such a small village as this.'

Old Irish saying: *'Sure he married her to get rid of her.'*

Dr Oliver Gogarty often told the story of two Englishmen fishing on a Connemara river. A local came along, put a worm on a bent pin and within a minute or two had caught a six-pound salmon. They watched with amazement as he measured it and threw it back before putting another worm on his line.

'Look,' said one of them, 'we don't mind you poaching, but why did you throw back that large fish?'

'Arrah,' said the local, 'bless your innocence, but sure my pan is only six inches across.'

A crazy young lad out of Slane,
Had some odd sort of thoughts on his brain.
   He swam the rivers of France,
   Led the gendarmes a dance,
And though guilty they found him in Seine.

The old lady picked a winner almost every day of the week and
the bookie was curious.
   'How do you do it, Mrs Casey?'
   'I stick a pin in the paper and that's how.'

Mrs Redmond went into the confession box and was about to
start when she noticed an unfamiliar face behind the shutter.
   'You're not Father Donlon. What are you doing there?'
   'I'm the french polisher, M'am.'
   'Well, where is Father Donlon?'
   'I couldn't tell you, but if he heard anything like the stories
I've been listening to, he's gone for the police.'

*An Englishman thinks seated; a Frenchman, standing; an American,
pacing; and an Irishman, afterwards.*

The American tourist was looking over Phelim's farm.

'How many acres have you got?' he asked.

'About thirty,' Phelim said proudly.

'You know,' the American went on, 'at home in Texas it takes me two days to drive around my ranch.'

'Poor you,' sympathised Phelim. 'I had a car like that wanst but I sold it.'

Pat was not accustomed to the thin bread of his London boarding-house.

'Did you cut them yourself?' he asked the landlady pointing to the heap of slices.

'I did, Pat.' she answered.

'All right then, I'll shuffle and deal.'

There was an old person of Newry,
Whose wife was a *lusus naturae,*
  Though outwardly pleasant,
  When others were present,
The sight of her drove him to fury.

An Irish bull has been described as a short cut along the road of mental quickness. Instead of keeping to the main road of logic it skips across the fields and cuts off the miles. For instance a Dublin cinema attendant was once asked what business was like, 'To tell you the truth,' he said, 'when the place isn't half-full, it's half-empty.'

It was a bitter election campaign and Murphy felt he should speak to his rival, O'Growney, about the whole thing.

'Look, O'Growney,' he said, 'we'll have to improve this campaign. Sure we'll have to make it clean. For a start I'll promise to tell no more lies about you.'

'Good,' answered O'Growney, 'and I'll give you my solemn word not to tell the truth about you.'

Fursa O'Siochain was a newcomer to wealth, and when he turned up for his first hunt meeting he was wearing only one spur. O'Reilly thought he'd put him right.

'Fursa,' he whispered, 'you're only wearing one spur.'

'Ah, sure, O'Reilly, only one is needed. If one side of the horse goes the other is sure to follow along.'

The salesman persuaded Mrs Cassey that his ointment would clear up the warts on her husband's face. Two days later she was back looking for a refund.

'Did it not clear up his face?' asked the salesman.

'It did indeed. The warts are still there but his face is gone.'

The Co. Donegal farmer was convinced he'd swallowed a horse and he couldn't be persuaded otherwise. Eventually they got him to a psychiatrist who gave him an injection, put him to sleep and brought a big white gelding to the bedside.

'There you are, Finnegan. I removed the horse.'

Finnegan shook his head sadly.

''Tis fooling me you are. Sure my horse is a Connemara pony.'

> Horace Beatty from fair Ballyneety,
> Dined a cannibal chief, oh so meaty,
> He did the courteous thing,
> And toasted the king,
> Who didn't take long to toast Beatty.

The family gathered around the baptismal font and the ceremony commenced.

'And now,' said the priest, 'what name are you giving the child?'

'Patrick Eamonn Sean Fergus Oscar Phelim Michael Pascal Xavier Thomas,' announced the proud god-mother.

The priest turned to the altar boy: 'Quick, get more Holy Water.'

She was shocked with the maid.

'Marie,' she said, 'I find your bra hanging from the light and your slip on the fridge and I'm told you did a striptease for my son. Is it indeed true that while I was absent you entertained him here last night?'

'Well, I hope so, Mam . . . I did me best.'

It was the old man's 105th birthday and all the reporters of Co. Mayo gathered around with the same old question: 'How do you account for your long life?'

'Vitamin pills,' the old man cackled.

'Vitamin pills?' they cried.

'Yus,' mumbled the ancient one. 'I haven't missed them for a day since I turned the century.'

The greyhound was a grave disappointment to everyone in Thurles and they lost a fortune on him.

'There's only one thing that will improve that dog, Paudeen,' urged a neighbour. 'Put some lead in his left ear.'

'And sure how would I do that?' asked Paudeen.

'With a shotgun!'

Then there was the Spiddal man with two wooden legs whose house went on fire. He was burnt to the ground.

Mulligan and Company had been slow in delivering the goods, so Michael Fahy sent them a telegram telling them to cancel his order. A reply came very rapidly. *'Cannot cancel your order at once. You will have to wait your turn.'*

They were so busy playing the duet they didn't notice the tinker looking in the window.

'Hey, why did you come out of there without seeing if you could get help?' asked his indignant wife.

'Don't be mad, woman,' he answered. 'They're so poor that two of them has to play the one piano.'

She didn't approve of smoking and when the newcomer got into the carriage and lit his pipe she couldn't help letting him know.

'Do you know that my husband is sixty years of age and he never put a pipe in his mouth?'

'M'am, I'm sixty-five and never put it anywhere else.'

The new farm labourer was from the city and didn't know too much about the work. He had been milking for some time when the farmer went along to see how he was doing. To his surprise the labourer was feeding the cow with milk.

'What in the name of the Seven holy men of Pogmohone are you doing?'

'The cow dropped its dirty tail in the pail and I'm putting the milk through her again.'

A beautiful blonde of Kilbride,
Went along in a bus for the ride.
    The conductor's 'Your fare,'
    Was said with a glare.
'No, I'm not,' she just grinned, 'I've been dyed.'

In Miami the local was explaining to Seamus the time-lag between Ireland and the United States.

'Look at it this way, Seamus, while we're lying here in the sun all the folks at home are asleep in bed.'

Seamus shook his head bitterly: 'There you are again. No justice for Ireland.'

'Mick, I'm after knocking down the ladder!'

'Well, go and tell the foreman as quick as you can.'

'Sure he knows.'

'Are you certain?'

'Certain, didn't I leave him hanging from the gutter when the ladder fell?'

The short-sighted Trinity professor was thrilled when his first shot brought down something in the distance.

'What,' he cried, 'is the name of the species I have successfully shot!'

'Well,' said his beater, 'between curses he says his name is Murphy.'

And there was that Dublin householder who rushed the decoration of his home so that he'd have it finished before the pot of paint ran out.

Winston Churchill once travelled on the Tralee–Ballybunion railway. The train stopped at one station and showed no sign of moving. Winston asked a porter if anything could be done to get the journey under way again and mentioned who he was.

'Look, sir, if you were the station master's son, it wouldn't make any difference.'

An Irishman was caught by cannibals on one occasion and finding that his blood was almost pure alcohol they drew off a pint each day for the chief. He got fed up in the end with this and put his foot down: 'Ate me if you want to, you hungry gombeen men, but stop sticking me for drinks.'

He was returning from London after a year in exile. His two brothers were at the crossroads to meet him and the first thing he noticed was their long beards.

'Mick . . . Colum! What did you grow beards for at all?'

Colum shuffled angrily.

'Sure what did you expect? Didn't you take the bloody razor blade with you?'

A silly young girl of Knockcroghery,
Was asked to make love in a roghery,
   She said, 'It's not nice,
   Amid edelweiss,
In fact it's no more than a moghery!'

'If you feed hens different foods it will effect the eggs,' explained the Agricultural adviser to the farmer.

'I know that,' replied Flaherty; 'a cousin of mine in America fed his hens sawdust and when the eggs were hatched six of the chickens had wooden legs and four of them were woodpeckers.'

The Glasgow landlady had served Eoin his herrings in a very watery sauce and he didn't touch it.

'Och, why·are ye no eatin' yer fash?' asked Mrs McIntosh.

'To tell you the truth, Missus, I'm waitin' for the tide to go out a piece . . .'

They were holding hands at the pigsty in the sheltering shadow of the manure heap.

'I tell you, Cait, I bet you've been out with worse lookin' fellas nor me.'

Silence.

'I said, Cait, that I bet you've been out with . . .'

'Shut up. I'm thinking.'

The characters odd of Sam Beckett,
Are dreary and dull but can't check it.
    In bins and in sand,
    They eternally stand,
And meaning and sense, why they wreck it.

Lost between decks on the great Atlantic liner only an hour after putting to sea, McCormick had to look for help to find his cabin.

'What was the number?' asked the steward.

'I couldn't tell you,' said McCormick, 'but I'd know it because it had a lighthouse outside the porthole.'

The happy-go-lucky Irish maid was about to serve her first dinner.

'And Nuala,' said the lady of the house, 'you must make absolutely certain that you serve from the left and take away from the right.'

'Lord, Ma'am, aren't you awful superstitious.'

'How do you like my cow?' asked the farmer as he showed his stock to a young Dublin girl.

'She's nice, but isn't it a funny place she has her fingers?'

The tinker was in court charged with stealing an overcoat.

'My man,' said the District Justice, 'three years ago you were before me charged also with stealing an overcoat.'

'Of course,' said the tinker. 'How long do you think overcoats last?'

'Could you lend me the price of two pints of Guinness,' he pleaded.

'The price of two pints? Now wouldn't the price of one be enough for you.'

'Do you think I'm mean,' came the indignant reply, 'sure you'll have to have one on me.'

> A stupid young boyo of Naas,
> Had a most vacant look on his face,
>   So his friends for a bet,
>   Put a notice 'To Let,'
> Now an ad. for girls' socks fills the place.

'When I was on holiday in Galway I stayed in a very nice hotel in Athlone.'

'Sure you're crazy. Athlone is about sixty miles from Galway.'

'Is it indeed! No wonder it took me so long to walk to the beach.'

The Kerryman had a remarkable range of general knowledge and the visitor asked him how he knew so much.

'This is the way of it,' he said; 'I picked up a bit here and I picked up a bit there and I was too lazy to forget it.'

They were making a match, but the farmer's son wasn't too happy.

'But, da,' he protested, 'The girl has a shockin' limp.'

'It's a wife you're marryin',' growled the father, 'not a bloody show jumper.'

Although they were amateurs the Wexford farmer took a chance and lent them two guns and three dogs. Half-an-hour later they were back.

'What do you want?' he asked, 'More ammunition?'

'Oh, no. More dogs.'

Colm had returned to his native town after many years abroad.

'I hope,' said his parish priest, 'that you have been loyal to your faith while you've been away?'

'Indeed, Father, I have. I lied, I fought, I cursed, I robbed and I had women but not for one moment did I foret the religion I was brought up in.'

> 'Oh, sweet mistress mine of Listowel,
> I love you heart, body and sowel.
> If your teeth were your own.
> And your shape not a cone,
> I'd say you'd be nice on the whowel.'

Mrs Hennessy met an old school chum in Paris and decided to impress her.

'You know,' she sighed with an air of deprivation, 'we've been here a week and I haven't been to the Louvre yet.'

Her friend lifted a shocked eyebrow.

'Well, don't wait any more, see a doctor.'

She followed her husband to the public-house.

'How can you come here,' she said, taking a sip of his pint of stout, 'and drink that awful stuff?'

'Now!' he cried, 'And you always said I was just out enjoying myself.'

'Mary,' complained the mistress to her new maid from the country, 'I can write my name on the dust on the piano.'

'Oh, Mam, isn't it wonderful to have the education,' marvelled Mary.

Brendan Behan told the story of how he got a job in London with a street repair gang. The first job he went to they were down in a hole singing *Happy Birthday* around the foreman.

'Is it the foreman's birthday?' asked Brendan.

'No, Brendan. It's the third anniversary of the hole.'

The racehorse owner was annoyed with the running of his horse at the Curragh. He turned on the jockey.

'Flaherty, could you not have raced faster?'

'Of course I could, boss, but you know we're supposed to stay on the horses.'

'I've been told of the bird and the bee,'
Said a sweet little rose of Tralee.
  'Their ways are so strange,
  I could never arrange,
To let anyone try it with me.'

The doctor stood up.

'I'm afraid, Mrs Tighe, your husband is dead.'

'I am not,' came a feeble but defiant voice from the bed.

His wife turned on him.

'Houl' your tongue. The doctor knows better than youse.'

The three thugs attacked Slattery and it was a fierce struggle. Finally they got him down and took three shillings and a halfpenny from his pocket.

'What the hell did you put up a fight like that for three shillings and a halfpenny?' asked one of the disgusted hijackers.

'Sure I thought you were after the ten pound note in me sock.'

The two tinkers were making camp for the night.

'Yerra, man, what do you want with that length of drainpipe you're carrying?'

'Tis I'm going to use it for a pillow.'

'Sure t'would be as hard as the hob of hell.'

'Is it a fool you take me for? I'm going to stuff it with straw first

'Excuse me, sir,' said the farm labourer to his boss, 'I've been watching the bull chase your wife around the meadow for the past hour.'

'You fool, why didn't you tell me before.'

'Why? Does she get tired quickly?'

An Irishman was in the dock for drunkenness.

'Where did you get the money to buy all that whiskey,' asked the District Justice.

'My friend Haggis McTavish gave it to me.'

'Three months for perjury,' rapped the judge.

Then there was the little boy who wanted his hair cut the same way as his Daddy's with the hole in the top for his head to come through.

An elegant dandy from Cork,
Hand on hip took a stroll through the pork.
    He won glances so queer,
    They filled him with fear,
And he took to his bed with the shork.

J. P. Mahaffy, the Irish wit and scholar, was once involved in a
tedious argument on the social inequalities of women.
    'After all, Mahaffy, what is the difference between you and a
woman?'
    'I cannot conceive,' was the suave reply.

The farmer and his son were both lazy. As they sprawled in their
chairs one day the father said:
    'Paudeen, go out and see if it's raining.'
    'Ah sure can't you call in the dog and see if he's wet?'

    The tourist found himself at the railway station and thought
he would make conversation with the old porter.
    'Tell me,' he asked, 'where does this railway line go?'
    'Nowhere. Sure it's been in the one place all my life.'

Mrs Mulligan was delighted with the letter from her son who
had emigrated to London.
    'He has a great job,' she boasted to her neighbours. 'The best.
He's working in a crematorium burning Englishmen and getting
paid for it.'

Long courtships are notorious in Ireland and after a fifteen-year
courtship Shaun went to see the father of his girl.
    'I've been going with your daughter now, Mr Cummisky,
for fifteen years.'
    'You have indeed, Shaun.'
    'D'ye think there'd be any objection if I married her?'
    'Certainly, Shaun,' said the relieved father. 'For a moment
there I thought you were going to ask for a pension.'

A bell-ringer bold in Kilkeel,
Made all of the local girls reel,
    When asked how was this,
    He said that each Miss,
Could be won to his side by a peal.

The lecturer was proud of his ancestry and he didn't conceal it from his County Cork audience.

'I was born an Englishman; I live as an Englishman and I hope to die an Englishman.'

'Yerra,' came a loud voice from the back of the hall,' have ye no ambition in ye at all?'

The reporters as usual were gathered around the centenarian.

'To what, Mr Grogan, do you attribute your great age.'

'The Irish climate.'

'You mean it's healthy?'

'No, but t'would put years on you.'

As elsewhere there are some people in Ireland who look on insurance as a source of income rather than protection. It happened in Limerick one time.

'Clancy, my poor fella, I'm powerful sorry to hear about your shop being burned down last Tuesday.'

'Shut up will you . . . that's next Tuesday.'

Mary and John decided to buy a car after many years and they went into the dealer to pay for it. John threw two socks on the counter.

'There you are,' he said, 'there's £500 in one pound notes in these.'

'Come over, Macauley, we've a party,' said Carthy on the phone.

'I can't go. We have a bad case of laryngitis here.'

'Heck, bring it over—we'll drink anything.'

A bald-headed fool of Kilmead,
Rubbed his skull with a mixture of seed.
   In the end, stupid ass,
   He was covered with grass,
So they hoed him each day to find weed.

After each drink Murphy took a frog from his pocket, put it on
the bar counter and stared at it. Eventually the barman asked him
what he was up to.

   'You see,' said Murphy, 'so long as I can see one frog I'm sober.
It's when I see two that I have to do something.'

   'And what do you do?'

   'I pick up the two of them, put them in my pocket and g.
home.'

The tinker whined outside the farmer's door.
   'Give us twopence for a bed, sir.'
   'Let me see it first.'

*If all the world's economists, quipped George Bernard Shaw,
were laid end to end they wouldn't even reach a conclusion.*

Tadgh took a correspondence course in body-building and
finished in three months. He wrote to the school: 'I have now
finished the course. Please send on the muscles by return.'

A neurotic girl from Kilbane,
Once kissed every man on a train.
  Saying, 'My nerves it'll cure,
  But can I endure,
The boredom of being too sane?'

The Wicked Landlord had robbed the poor farmer's daughter of her Virtue but he wanted to be just. He sent for the mother of the girl to come to him.

'Mrs O'Shaughnessy, you must know I can't marry your daughter but I wish to compensate her. I'll settle five thousand pounds on the child and give a further two thousand pounds to your daughter. For yourself, I have five hundred pounds.'

She was left a little breathless as she started to leave.

'The blessing of the revolving Indian saint of Inishbofin be on you, the blessing of the Holy Hermits of Clonmacnoise fall on you and all who belong to you . . .'

She paused as an awful thought struck her.

'Oh, heavens, sir . . . if she had a miscarriage will you give her another chance?'

'I'm going up to the Phoenix Park to tell something to my brother in the Three Day Bicycle Race.'

'Heavens, don't you know that ended two days ago?'

'I do. That's what I want to tell me brother.'

St Patrick was playing Moses on the heavenly links o paradise when he sank a hole in one. Moses teed up and with splendid skill sank another hole in one.

'Here,' said St Patrick, 'let's agree to cut out the miracles and play golf.'

'What were you saying to that man just now?'

'He wanted to give me the winner of the Irish Grand National.'

'And would you not take it?'

'Of course not, Sure we've only a very small garden.'

A professor who lived in Leixlip
Was forgetful when going on a trip.
   Confused and amiss,
   The porter he'd kiss,
And leave naught for his wife but a tip.

In rural Ireland there are spare-time barbers who shave and cut hair only on market days. Pierce had survived a rather close shave and, still shaking, he asked for a drink of water.

'What for, Pierce?'

'I want to see if my throat leaks.'

'Did you hear that I'm engaged to an Irish lad?'

'Oh, really!'

'No, O'Reilly.'

They rescued Shamus when he was on the brink of drowning and gave him the kiss of life and pumped him as dry as they could. When he was somewhat recovered they brought him a noble glass of smooth, rich Irish whiskey.

He looked at the drink and then asked reverently: 'Turn me over again lads and get more water out first.'

Poteen is an Irish illegal brew that can burn holes in steel plate. Oisin Flaherty after a pint of it saw so many animals in his room that he put a sign on his house 'Flaherty's Zoo.' The local Garda sergeant went to reason with him and was no sooner in than he was offered a glass of the Mountain Dew, as it is called. When he staggered out thirty minutes later he raised his hand for silence.

'Ish all right, men. The worst's over. He sold me half the elephants.'

A favourite Irish joke of P. G. Wodehouse tells of the English butler who served an aristocratic family during the 'Troubles' in the Green Isle. When they came to the great oak door their leader told the butler: 'We've come to shoot his Lordship. Get him.'

Imperturbably he replied: 'He's not here, sir; perhaps you could call again.'

The I.R.A. men burst into the house and set fire to everything they could burn. As they rushed out afterwards the butler was still standing with quiet dignity. He bowed as they swept by.

'Gentlemen,' he called after them, 'may I tell his Lordship who called?'

There was a young girl of Tralee,
Whose knowledge of French was, *'oui, oui.'*
　　Still gloriously praised,
　　Nightly glasses are raised,
To honour her memory in Paree.

There was the Cork farmer who won a large prize in a milking contest and told the reporters: 'I owe my success to udders.'

The letter from Sean to his old, old mother was heartening.

'Dear Mother,' he wrote, 'I am sending you some pills that a witch doctor gave me and if you take one it will take years off your life.'

He came home a few weeks later and there was a beautiful young woman outside his house rocking a pram in which a baby lay sucking a bottle.

'Where's me mother?' he asked.

'Arrah, don't be silly,' she said. 'I'm your mother and them pills were marvellous.'

'Imagine,' said Sean, 'one pill and you're as beautiful as anyone could be and what's more you were able to have a baby. Lord, but they were powerful.'

'You amadan,' she cried. 'That's not a baby – that's your father. He took two.'

'Paddy,' jeered the Yank as he pointed to two stone dogs on entrance piers to an estate, 'how often do you feed those animals?'

'Every time they bark,' grinned Paddy.

The tourist was in a great hurry but the only transport available to take him to the railway station was an old Irish sidecar. As they moved slowly along the tourist grew frantic.

'Hit that damn horse in a place he'll feel.'

'Peace,' said the driver; 'I've hit everywhere it hurts except the most important and I'm saving that for the big hill.'

A virile young boyo of Youghal,
Was renowned for his loud mating coughal,
   The sound of his voice,
   Made women rejoice,
In Kilbeggan, Athlone, Sligo, East Hampstead,
Duluth, Kells, Ontario, Tokyo, Ballydehob,
Washington, Little Neck, Cahirciveen, Galway
and, of course, St. Poughal.

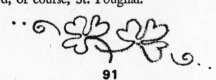